Ideal Parents

By
Shaykh Mufti Saiful Islām

JKN Publications

First Published in October 2017
ISBN: 978-1-909114-25-8

British Library Cataloguing in Publication Data
A catalogue record for this book is available from the British Library.

Publisher's Note:

Every care and attention has been put into the production of this book. If however, you find any errors, they are our own, for which we seek Allāh's ﷻ forgiveness and the reader's pardon.

Published by:

JKN Publications
118 Manningham Lane
Bradford
West Yorkshire
BD8 7JF
United Kingdom

t: +44 (0) 1274 308 456 | w: www.jkn.org.uk | e: info@jkn.org.uk

Book Title: Ideal Parents

Author: Shaykh Mufti Saiful Islām

Printed by Mega Printing in Turkey

"In the Name of Allāh, the Most Beneficent,
the Most Merciful"

Contents

Introduction

All Praises are due to Allāh ﷻ, the Sovereign and the Lord of the Worlds and may Peace, Blessings and Salutations be upon our Beloved Messenger, Muhammad ﷺ, upon his Noble Companions y, his family members and those who wholeheartedly follow his footsteps until the Last Hour. Āmīn!

Parenthood is the most challenging yet a crucial role in life. Its topic is of a fundamental importance in Islām. Despite the numerous hardships and worries one undergoes in fulfilling this important role, it is essential that all parents (or parents-to-be) first appreciate the blessings of parenthood and its rewards.

This book contains a selection of articles that have been taken from various social media avenues; magazines, emails and WhatsApp messages on the related topic and compiled into a book format in order to benefit parents. It presents a wealth of knowledge and guidance for parents in managing their responsibilities and tips to overcoming challenging situations. The book aims to inspire parents through beneficial advices and real life accounts, offering them some hope in this lifelong responsibility through implementation of those advices.

May Allāh ﷻ accept this compilation and benefit us from the knowledge, wisdom and advice contained within this book.

May He reward my beloved teacher and Shaykh, Shaykh Mufti Saiful Islām Sāhib for all his efforts and bestow countless blessings upon his family and loved ones in this world and the Hereafter. Āmīn!

Palwasha Ustrana
Student of Jāmiah Khātamun Nabiyeen (Rotherham)
August 2017/Dhul-Qa'dah 1438

What to do after a Child is Born

Every married couple want to experience parenthood. When Allāh ﷻ fulfils this wish, we should forever remain grateful towards Him by following the guidelines of our beloved Prophet ﷺ. The Tarbiyah of our children begins from birth which the Prophet ﷺ has demonstrated. This will bring blessings and Barakah throughout the life of the new born Inshā-Allāh.

Adhān

The first practice which should be carried out is Adhān in the right ear and Iqāmat in the left ear. Sayyidunā Abū Rāfi ؓ says, "I saw the Prophet ﷺ giving Adhān in the ears of Sayyidunā Hasan ؓ when he was born." (Tirmizi)

The wisdom behind this is that the first words which enter the baby's ears are the words of Allāh ﷻ. This is to instill submission and worship to Allāh ﷻ Alone in the child and the final Prophethood of the Noble Messenger ﷺ.

Tahnīk

The term Tahnīk means placing of a piece of date, which is softened by chewing by a pious person on the palate of the new born. The practice of Tahnīk is Sunnah.

It is narrated that Sayyidunā Abdullāh Ibn Zubair ؓ was brought to the Holy Prophet ﷺ and the Holy Prophet ﷺ did Tahnīk, prayed for him and blessed him. (Bukhāri)

In another narration it is reported, "New-born children would be brought to the Messenger of Allāh ﷺ and he would supplicate for them and rub a chewed date upon their palate." (Muslim)

Imām Nawawi ﷺ says, "Scholars are unanimous upon the recommendation of performing Tahnīk upon the baby after its birth." The purpose of Tahnīk is that the first item that should enter a baby's mouth is the saliva of the pious.

Note: The date should be prepared, softened and chewed prior to the labour. The method of placing the date on the baby's palate should be learnt before-hand.

Sunnats to be Performed on the Seventh Day after the Child's Birth

1. Removing the hair of the child:
It is Sunnah to remove the baby's hair. The hair should be weighed and an equivalent amount of silver should be donated to charity. It is stated in a Hadīth that when Sayyidunā Hasan ﷺ was born, the Prophet ﷺ instructed his daughter, Sayyidah Fātimah ﷺthus, "Shave his head and give the weight of his hair in silver to the poor."

(Ahmad)

The hair being an aspect of the human body should be buried due to respect.

2. Applying saffron to a child's head.

The Prophet ﷺ instructed us to apply Khalūq on the child's head'.
(Abū Dāwūd)

'Khalūq' is the name of a fragrance made from a combination of saffron and other ingredients.

This Sunnah is to be carried out in the following manner; Place saffron in a bowl of water. Dip hands into this water and apply it to the baby's head.

3. Aqīqah

After the arrival of the new baby, it is also Sunnah to slaughter an animal; sheep or goat. If the new born is a boy then sacrificing two animals is recommended and for a girl only one animal will suffice. (Those animals which are permissible to slaughter on Eidul Adhā are also allowed in Aqīqah). Sayyidah Āishah ﷺ narrates that the Holy Prophet ﷺ instructed us to sacrifice two goats in favour of a boy and one goat for a girl (Tirmizi). It is also desirable to perform Aqīqah in the country where the child is born. One should consume the meat of Aqīqah, but it is desirable to divide the meat into three portions; one for the poor and two-thirds for friends and family. This meat can be distributed cooked or raw.

4. Circumcision

To perform Khatnah (circumcision) of a male child on the seventh day after the child's birth has been recommended otherwise any day is permissible.

Congratulating New Parents

It is Mustahab (recommended) to congratulate the new parents upon the birth of their child and to supplicate for them and their child.
This adds to their happiness and creates an atmosphere of love and
unity. The Holy Qur'ān refers to glad tidings (Bashāra) given to Sayyidunā Ibrāhīm ﷺ and Sayyidunā Zakariyya ﷺ. Allāh ﷻ says regarding Sayyidunā Ibrāhīm ﷺ:

فَبَشَّرْنَاهُ بِغُلَامٍ حَلِيمٍ

**"So, We gave him (Ibrāhīm) the good news of a forbearing
boy." (37:101)**

In reference to Sayyidunā Zakariyya ﷺ, Allāh ﷻ says,

يَازَكَرِيَّا إِنَّا نُبَشِّرُكَ بِغُلَامٍ اسْمُهُ يَحْيٰى ...

**"O' Zakariyyā, We give you the good news of a boy whose name
is Yahyā..." (19:7)**

The above verses refer to Allāh ﷻ giving glad tidings to two of His
Prophets. There is a technical difference between Bishāra and congratulating (Tahni'a), in that the former means to notify someone of
good news which he was unaware of previously, whilst the latter refers to making Du'ā and congratulating someone who is aware of the
news. However, the notion is the same in both; that is, to express
happiness due to the good news. (Ibnul Qayyim - Tuhfatul-Mawlūd)

11

Abū Burdah ﷺ relates from Sayyidunā Abū Mūsā ﷺ that he said, "A son was born to me, so I took him to the Messenger of Allāh ﷺ. He named him Ibrāhīm, placed (some part of a) date in his mouth after chewing it (Tahnīk), supplicated for Allāh's ﷺ blessing upon him and then gave him back to me..." (Bukhāri)

In view of the above and other evidences, many classical scholars such as Imām Nawāwi ﷺ and Ibnul Qayyim ﷺ state that it is recommended to congratulate and supplicate (make Du'ā) upon the birth of a child. Imām Ibnul Qayyim ﷺ states, "If one is unable to give glad-tidings, it is Mustahab to congratulate them." (Tuhfatul-Mawlūd)

As such, one should congratulate the parents and family, irrespective of whether the new born is a boy or girl. One should supplicate to Allāh ﷺ that He blesses the child, makes them righteous, make them a means of coolness for their parent's eyes, gives them good health and guides the parents towards gratefulness.

Some specific supplications have also been reported in this regard,

1. Hasan Basri ﷺ advised a man to supplicate with the following words when congratulating new parents:

بَارَكَ اللهُ لَكَ فِى الْمَوْهُوْبِ لَكَ، وَشَكَرْتَ الْوَاهِبَ، وَبَلَغَ أَشُدَّه، وَرُزِقْتَ بِرَّه

"May Allāh bless you in His gift to you, may you give thanks to the Bestower of this gift, may the child reach the maturity of years and may you be granted its righteousness."

Both Imām Nawāwi ﷺ in his Al-Adhkār and Imām Ibnul Qayyim ﷺ in his Tuhfatul-Mawlūd relate this Du'ā from Hasan Basri ﷺ. It was originally reported by Ibnul-Ja'd in his Musnad, Ibn Abi Dunyā, Abū Bakr Ibnul Mundhir in his Al-Awsat and Ibn Adi in his Al-Kāmil.

Imām Nawāwi ﷺ states that, it is also recommended for the one being congratulated, i.e. the new parents, to respond with the following or a similar Du'ā:

بَارَكَ اللهُ لَكَ، وبَارَكَ عَلَيْكَ، وجَزَاكَ اللهُ خَيْرًا، ورَزَقَكَ اللهُ مِثْلَه، وأَجْزَلَ ثَوَابَكَ

"May Allāh ﷻ bless you and shower His blessings upon you; and may Allāh ﷻ reward you with good, grant you the same and increase your reward."

2. Abū Ayyūb As-Sakhtiyāni ﷺ the great Imām, would congratulate new parents with the following supplication:

جَعَلَهُ اللهُ مُبَارَكًا عَلَيْكَ وَعَلَى أُمَّةِ مُحَمَّدٍ صَلَّى اللهُ عَلَيْهِ وَسَلَّمَ

"May Allāh ﷻ make the child a blessing for you and a blessing for the Ummah of Muhammad ﷺ."

Imām Tabarāni ﷺ and others record from Abū Ayyūb As-Sakhtiyāni ﷺ; Tabarāni also reports this from Imām Hasan Basri ﷺ.

3. Giving Gifts

Giving gifts to the parents and to the new born is also a good way of fostering friendship and love. However, it must be remembered that giving gifts must not become a mere custom and they must not be expected or considered as obligatory.

The Wife of the Caliph Nurses a Pregnant Woman

It was the custom of Sayyidunā Umar Ibn Khattāb ◌, the Leader of the Believers to patrol at night looking after the needs of the people and to make sure that everyone was safe. As he passed by an open area in Madīnah Munawwarah, he heard the moans of a woman coming out from a small and shabby house, at the door of which a man was seated. Sayyidunā Umar ◌ greeted him and asked him how he was. The man said that he was from the desert and had come seeking to reap some generosity from the Leader of the Believers. Sayyidunā Umar ◌ asked him about the reason for the woman moaning. The man, not knowing that he was speaking to the Leader of the Believers, said, "Go away, may Allāh ◌ have mercy on you, and do not ask about that which does not concern you."

However, Sayyidunā Umar ◌ persisted in asking the same question, offering to help if he could. So the man informed him, "Indeed she is my wife who is about to give birth, yet, there is no one here to help her."

Sayyidunā Umar ؓ left the man, rushed to his house and woke up his wife, Sayyidah Umm Kulthūm ؅, and said to her, "Will you accept the reward that Allāh ﷻ has brought to you?" She said, " What is that goodness and reward, O' Amīrul Mu'minīn?"

No sooner did he inform her of what happened, that she stood up and took all that she needed to help the woman deliver her baby and all that the new born would need as well. Meanwhile, the Leader of the Believers took a pot and with it some fat and grains. He and his wife hurried off together until they reached the same shabby house. While Sayyidah Umm Kulthūm ؅ went in to help the pregnant woman, the Leader of the Believers remained outside with the husband, and cooked the food that he brought with him.

From inside the house, Sayyidah Umm Kulthūm ؅ called out, "O' Amīrul Mu'minīn, give glad tidings to your companion that Allah ﷻ has bestowed him with a baby boy."

The man was amazed to find out that it was the Leader of the Believers who was seated with him and who was cooking food for him and the wife was shocked to learn that it was the wife of the Leader of the Believers who came to meet her and help her in her shabby house.

I'm Not Religious Enough to Teach my Kids

وَلْتَكُنْ مِنْكُمْ أُمَّةٌ يَّدْعُوْنَ إِلَى الْخَيْرِ وَيَأْمُرُوْنَ بِالْمَعْرُوْفِ وَيَنْهَوْنَ عَنِ الْمُنْكَرِ وَأُولَٰئِكَ هُمُ الْمُفْلِحُوْنَ

"There should be a group from you, who invite towards good (in religion) and command what is right and forbid evil. These are indeed the successful ones." (3:104)

Do you ever think you cannot advise your children about something because you are not practicing it yourself? This issue is not limited to just religion, but this is where the doubt in one's mind feels the strongest.

Smokers know it makes sense to warn kids about the dangers of smoking, but why do we feel so ashamed to teach to a level higher than what we may practice at home, in terms of religion? The command from Allāh ﷻ in the Holy Qur'ān to invite to good and forbid the evil says nothing about 'the good that you do and the evil you abstain from.'

Many wish they were a better example for their kids and many have had to fight the urge to leave their Islamic studies behind because we have had to get past the embarrassment of teaching to a higher standard than we practice. There are things we do right, but how do we get past our own shortcomings?

A Shaykh once mentioned that even if we do not practice ourselves, the least we can do is educate and instil the love of Allāh ﷻ in our children so they will, Inshā-Allāh, pray for us and be a source of good deeds. As our children get older, who knows? Maybe, they will be a good influence on us as well.

Just like we teach our children to have higher goals in schooling and make better choices than we made in our youth, then why should it be so difficult on teaching kids religion just because we have not been practicing to the level we may feel in our hearts?

Inshā-Allāh, we can at least give our children a solid foundation of knowledge so they know how to connect with Allāh ﷻ, despite the shortcomings on the part of the parents.

How to Inspire Manners in your Children

1. When entering the house, greet your children with Salām and kisses. This should help develop their sense of love and mercy.

2. Be good to your neighbours. Never backbite or speak ill of anyone in front of them. Your children listen, absorb and emulate.

3. When calling your parents, encourage your children to speak to them. When visiting you parents, take your children with you. The more they see you take care of your parents, the more they will learn to take care of you.

4. When driving them to school, don't always play albums or CD's. Rather, tell them the stories yourself. This will have a greater impact - trust me!

5. Read to them a short Hadīth, once a day – it doesn't take much time, but very impactful in creating strong bonds and wonderful memories.

6. Comb your hair, clean your teeth and wear presentable clothes even if sitting at home and not going out for the day. They need to learn that being clean and tidy has nothing to do with going out!

7. Try not to blame or comment on every word or action they say or do. Learn to overlook and let go of things. This certainly builds their self-confidence.

8. Ask your children's permission before entering their rooms. Don't just knock and enter, but wait for verbal permission. They will learn to do the same when wanting to enter your room.

9. Apologise to your children if you made a mistake. Apologizing teaches them to be humble and polite.

10. Don't be sarcastic or make fun of their views or feelings, even if you "didn't mean it" and was "only joking". It really hurts.

11. Show respect to your children's privacy. It's important for their sense of value and self-esteem.

12. Don't expect that they will listen or understand the first time. Don't take it personally. Our Holy Prophet ﷺ never did. But be patient and consistent.

13. Never call them names by which they become offended e.g stupid, fatso, daft and so forth. This makes them feel worthless and demoralises them.

14. Always appreciate their efforts. Do not reprimand them if they don't attain first position in school or Madrasah. The important thing is that they are hard working.

15. Every time you speak with your children, speak with respect. Say things like, "Thank you," etc. Don't use slang i.e. 'gimmi,' instead say 'please give me'; use clear words, be polite and never swear.

16. You need to bear in mind that children always like to play. Never take away their playing time by treating them like an adult.

17. Assist your children to make decisions. He or she must be taught to make decisions. Acknowledge them, guide them by talking to them.

18. There is nothing wrong in consulting your child now and then in certain matters. Consulting them makes them feel special.

19. Teach your child to follow you in Salāh. Lead them rather than instructing them. This is more effective. Children always remember what you do and what you say. Start instructing them to read Salāh at the age of seven, this will help them and make it easy for them to follow when they reach puberty, when it becomes compulsory on them.

20. Teach your children how to put forward their opinion, how you would disagree to a point. Do not use swear words when you disagree on anything. This will inculcate in your child as he is watching you being aggressive. Children have much more grasping power than us and they pick up things very fast.

21. Never reproach your children if they ask you a question for information. Appreciate it as they chose to come to you rather than anyone else. Explain according to their level. If its beyond their level then mention it to them.

22. Always fulfil your promises towards your children. Do not make big promises which you cannot fulfil otherwise this makes them develop a habit of making false promises.

23. Teach your children how to develop skills in becoming good team member. This encourages them to give chances to others rather than always competing.

24. Make Du'ā for your children even if they have gone astray.

25. Tell them you might fail once, but never lose hope. Teach them how they should react to failure.

26. Apologise to your child if you have made a mistake. This teaches your child to repent to Allāh ﷻ. Do not raise 'ifs' and 'buts' when you are wrong. There are no 'ifs' and 'buts' when it comes to repentance.

27. Have a few surprises for your children. Praise them for their good deed. Give them recognition at home that this surprise is for doing such and such good thing.

28. Train your children to read a portion of the Holy Qur'ān daily according to their capacity.

29. Tell your children repeatedly that you love them. Tell them how gorgeous they look and how important they are to you. Hug them and kiss them as this is Sunnah.

A Beautiful Approach to Teaching Islamic Knowledge to our Children

A woman narrates a marvellous story and says, "I was on a visit to one of my friend's house. One of her daughters, who was about three years old, came in, stood behind her and pulled on her dress saying, "Mum, we did not build a house in Jannah today." I thought I misheard her. Then, her siblings joined her and they all repeated the same thing. My friend saw the curiosity on my face and smiled and said to me: "Do you want to see how we build a mansion in Jannah?" I stood and watched as the mother and her children sat around her and recited Sūrah Al-Ikhlās ten times.

$$ قُلْ هُوَ اللّٰهُ أَحَدٌ ۚ اللّٰهُ الصَّمَدُ ۚ لَمْ يَلِدْ وَلَمْ يُولَدْ ۚ وَلَمْ يَكُنْ لَّهٗ كُفُوًا أَحَدٌ $$

When they finished, they all said excitedly with one voice: Alhamdulillāh, we built a house in Paradise. Then the mother asked: "What do you want to add to this palace?" The children replied that they wanted to add treasures. Then they began chanting,

$$ لَا حَوْلَ وَلَا قُوَّةَ اِلَّا بِاللّٰهِ $$

Then she asked them, "Which of you wants to drink from the hands of the Prophet ﷺ and never feel thirsty again?" They all began to say the Durūd Sharīf,

اللهم صل على محمد وعلى آل محمد كما صليت على إبراهيم وعلى آل إبراهيم
إنك حميد مجيد اللهم بارك على محمد وعلى آل محمد كما باركت على إبراهيم
وعلى آل إبراهيم إنك حميد مجيد

They followed it with praising Allāh ﷻ. Then, each of them went back to what they were doing from studying and playing with toys.

I asked her, "How did you do that?" She replied, "My children love sitting with me and rejoice when I gather them and sit among them. I take full advantage of it and teach them how to praise and thank Allāh ﷻ in a way that their tiny minds can understand. They see palaces in children's programs and wish to live in them, and watch cartoon heroes who are struggling to get treasures.

This mother will be rewarded with deeds whenever her children recite these Adhkār. It will be an ongoing charity. It is the best investment in this world and the Hereafter.

Islamic educational style is beautiful. Teach it to your children and spread it everywhere.

Advice for Parents of Hifz Students

Memorising the entire Qur'ān is a dream many Muslim parents to-day have for their children. Indeed, this is a goal nobler than any-thing else. However, after children have memorised a number of Sūrahs and perhaps even a Juzz or two of the Holy Qur'ān, there is a question that plagues many parents: How do I know if my child is ready to commit to memorising the entire Qur'ān and how well does he remember it?

Parents should be aware that doing Hifz of the Holy Qur'ān is not an easy task. It requires a tremendous effort, focus and dedication on behalf of the student, parents and the teacher. Therefore, when de-ciding whether or not to enrol your children in a Hifz class, make sure that you, the child and the teacher are prepared for this huge and blessed commitment.

If the child has a Qur'ān teacher, ask the teacher if she/he feels your child is capable of doing Hifz of the Holy Qur'ān. If the teacher thinks that the child indeed has the talent and dedication needed to memorise the Holy Qur'ān and that he/she does a very good job memorising Sūrahs, then you may consider enrolling the child in a Hifz class. However first you, the parent, must make sure that you are willing to expend the time and effort needed to support your child during this endeavour. If not, it may not be best to put this re-sponsibility on the child's shoulders.

Last, but not the least, children should have the commitment and enthusiasm to become a Hāfiz. Should they give up or unwilling to do it, then best to stop it altogether.

Unfortunately, many parents do not follow this advice given by Shaykh Zulfiqār Ahmad Naqshbandi, a very well-known and authentic scholar, Hāfiz and spiritual guide from Pakistan. Parents often force their children to do Hifz, when it is not Fardh (obligatory) on everyone to memorise the entire Qur'ān. Children should only be enrolled in a Hifz class if they are happy and willing to commit to this blessed task.

Okay, so you decided your child is ready to start Hifz. So what next?

After children are enrolled in a Hifz class, the children's parents and teachers should encourage them and teach them with love and compassion. When children are taught by someone with these characteristics, they reach ranks they never imagined.

In contrast, under no circumstances should the parents or the teachers beat their children for not memorising or not doing well on their lessons. When parents and teachers show children such harsh behaviour, there is a danger of them losing their interest to recite the Holy Qur'ān and their love for Islām. How many students are there who memorised the Holy Qur'ān under a harsh teacher and after completing the memorisation, stopped revising the Holy Qur'ān and later on abandoned what they worked so hard on? It is much better if a child willingly memorises half, or even a Juzz (part) of the Holy

Qur'ān rather than being beaten and forced into memorising the entire Holy Qur'ān.

The following are some additional things the parents of Hifz children can do to help them succeed:

Make Du'ā for your child. Parents' Du'ā for their children is extremely valuable and it is the best gift you can give them. Allāh ﷻ is the only One Who can truly help a person in any matter, which of course includes memorising His Blessed Words.

Help and Encourage Your Child to Abstain from Sins. Light and darkness cannot coexist in the same place. Similarly, by nature, the dazzling radiance of the Qur'ān and the darkness of sins simply cannot gather in one place. Engaging in sins such as watching movies, missing prayers, listening to music are displeasing to Allāh ﷻ. This has a detrimental impact on both the students' memorisation and on their connection with Allāh ﷻ. However, parents must admonish their children with affection to abstain from sins rather than through fear and force.

Be a Good Role Model. When your children see you reading the Qur'ān, they will very likely be encouraged to do the same, Inshā-Allāh. The same applies to praying Salāh, Allāh's ﷻ Dhikr (remembrance) etc. Engaging in acts of Ibādah strengthens a person's soul similar to the way food strengthens a person's body. A stronger soul will make it easier for your child to memorise the

Qur'ān, Inshā-Allāh.

Make Sure Your Child is Eating the Right Foods. It is crucial to make sure that your child consumes only Halāl foods. Consumption of Harām foods will negatively impact the child's progress in his or her memorisation of the Qur'ān. Also, make sure your child eats nutritious meals to maintain a balanced diet. Ensure that they eat a healthy breakfast every morning so to energise them.

Help Your Child Create a Schedule. It is necessary for Hifz students to devote at least a few hours every day for their memorisation . It is beneficial to create a set time for this task, as this will help to ensure that neither memorisation nor revision is over looked . The times after Fajr and Asr Salāh are very blessed for memorisation and revision. However, any time of the day that is convenient will work. Of course, even if the parents and teacher put their maximum effort into helping a student and yet, the student is not willing to strive to achieve his or her goal, then there will be very little progress.

Dear Parents

Tarzan lives half naked,

Cinderella comes home at midnight,

Pinocchio lies all the time,

Aladdin is the king of thieves,

Batman drives at 200 mph,

Romeo and Juliet commit suicide out of love,

Harry Potter uses witchcraft,

Mickey and Minnie are more than just friends,

Sleeping Beauty is lazy,
Dumbo gets drunk and hallucinated,

Scooby Doo gives nightmares,

And Snow White lives with seven guys.

We shouldn't be surprised if children misbehave, they get it from their storybooks and cartoons which "we" provide them.

We should instead be teaching them stories like:

Abū Bakr's ﷺ loyalty and undying service for his master,

Umar Ibn Khattāb's ﷺ love for justice and tolerance,

Uthmān Ibn Affān's ﷺ level of shyness and modesty,

Ali Ibn Abi-Tālib's ﷺ show of courage and bravery,

Khālid Ibn Walīd's ﷺ desire of combating evil,

Fātimah Bint Muhammad's ﷺ love and respect to her father,

Salāhuddīn Ayyūbi's ﷺ conquest of the promised land,
and many more to speak about.

Above all, we should teach them about Allāh ﷻ, the Qur'ān and the Sunnah with love, a very important aspect this is! And then see how the change begins Inshā-Allāh.

Faith Inspired Parenting

Years back, poor illiterate parents produced Doctors, Engineers, Scientists, Accountants, Lawyers, Architects and Professors whom we will refer to as Group 'A'.

These Group 'A' children struggled on their own after Year 6 or Year 12, to become notable personalities. Most of them walked to school, went to farms, fetched water and firewood, cared for the domesticated animals and did some work including trading after school to survive.

Now Group 'A' who have become parents themselves are producing Group 'B' children. These group B children are pampered, helped in their homework or home assignments, from nursery school through to secondary school to higher institutions.

They can watch movies from morning till dawn after school, they are treated like baby kings and queens, they don't do any household chores, they are given expensive cars and clothes, food is put on the table for them and their plates are removed and washed by parents or house maids. In spite of all this, only few can speak or write correctly.

The parents of Group 'A' cared for their own parents and children but Group 'B', their children are still struggling to find their feet at age thirty plus. They find it difficult to do things on their own because they are used to being helped to think and doing things by Group 'A'. So they can't help themselves, their parents or the society.

They abandon their parents to acquire the richness of this world.

Where do you belong?

Reduce the pampering and the unnecessary help you offer to your children. Let your children grow in wisdom, intelligence and strength.

Let them face the truth and the realities of life. Teach them to grow up in becoming independent adults. Teach them to fear Allāh ﷻ, respect others and develop confidence in themselves. Parents! Discipline your children to become disciplined adults, useful and not useless.

Never Curse Your Children!

'Angry mother's Du'ā made me Imām of Haram.'

Shaykh Al-Kalbāni, former Imām of the Ka'bah, at a conference in London was relating this story. When he was young, he was very naughty. He would make his mother very angry. But his mother, Allāh ﷻ bless her, was a very righteous woman who knew the power of Du'ā.

She made it her habit that, in her state of anger, she would say this Du'ā: "May Allāh ﷻ guide you and make you the Imām of the Ka'bah!"

Imām Al-Kalbāni told us, "So Allāh ﷻ answered her Du'ā, so I become one of the Imāms of the Ka'bah!"

Allāhū Akbar! The Shaykh being black and the son of a poor immigrant from the Persian Gulf now leads Salāh in Masjid Harām. In an interview with N.Y Times, Shaykh Kalbāni said, "Leading prayers at the Grand Mosque is an extraordinary honour, usually reserved for pure-blooded Arabs from the Saudi heartland."

He was taken aback when he came to know that King Abdullāh chose him as the first black Imām of Masjid Harām (in recent times), he added. Māshā-Allāh!

Don't curse your children when they misbehave. It will otherwise backfire!

Be careful with your words O' dear parents. Make it a habit to utter good Du'ās for them even when you're angry with them!

The Messenger of Allāh ﷺ said, "Three supplications will not be rejected (by Allāh ﷻ), the supplication of the parent for his child, the supplication of the one who is fasting and the supplication of the traveller." (Baihaqi, Tirmizi)

The Power of a Mother's Du'ā

When Imām Bukhāri ﷺ was three years of age, he lost his eyesight. His mother promised herself that she would pray Tahajjud Salāh until Allāh ﷻ restores her son's eyesight and that's exactly what she did.

She prayed Tahajjud every night until one night in a dream she saw Sayyidunā Ibrāhīm ﷺ giving her the good news that Imām Bukhāri's ﷺ eyesight has been restored. She rushed to her son and when he woke up, she found that his vision was restored.

Lessons for us:

This mother didn't go into a state of helplessness after her young child lost his eyesight. Being a single mother, she didn't lose hope and become disheartened with the difficulty she would have to face when bringing up her son with a disability. She knew the power behind every Du'ā and the beauty that lies in praying Tahajjud Salāh. It is during this time when Allāh ﷻ descends to the lowest heaven (in the manner which He knows best) asking His servants to make Duā to Him at this time. Her Taqwa, her conviction in the Might of Allāh ﷻ is what led her to consistently pray. To pray Tahajjud Salāh means you sacrifice your sleep which she did without fail.

When we read about the life of Imām Bukhāri ﷺ and his contribution towards Hadīth science, then take a look at the household he grew up in. It was due to his mother's nurturing of him and her Du'ā for him in the darkness of the night.

Imām Bukhāri's mother serves as an important lesson for us in how she managed with her difficulties. We should read about the lives of such women much as often, teaching us how to raise our own children Islamically, should we want our children to grow up to be righteous. An important reminder also, to never underestimate the power of Du'ā. Anything is possible with Du'ā.

Sacrifices of a Mother

Shaykh Umar Pālanpūri ﷺ talks about the sacrifices of his mother in his upbringing.

"As we entered early childhood, we saw our mother performing Salāh, making Du'ā and weeping profusely. In those days, our mother taught us the meaning and commentary of Sūrah Kahf (The Cave), which I can still remember until today. I remember her detailing the history of that wicked ruler in the Quranic Sūrah, Al-Burūj (The Towers) who had ordered the believers to be driven unto a ditch of fire.

One of her ways of reforming her children: Whenever she brought food from the market, she would give it to us so we divide it between ourselves. She would observe who was greedy among us and who was good hearted.

My mother wished for me to attain religious education, while the others favoured secular studies so to earn a descent livelihood. But my mother insisted that I study knowledge of Dīn. In doing so, the entire world would be under my feet. I wondered immaturely how a huge world could be under my feet.

Familiarising us with the religious ways by relating examples of the Prophets peace be upon them: To familiarize us with the religious ways, she would ask us to read out the story of Sayyidunā Mūsā u, Sayyidunā Yūsuf u and so on.

Once I was reading to her in the light of an oil lamp, as candles were expensive in those days, my mother said, "When a connection is established between Allāh ﷻ and His servant He fulfils whatever His servant beseeches." Then she said so passionately, "O' My son! Today I am listening to you in this dimly lighted house, may Allāh ﷻ cause hundreds and thousands to listen to you one day."

Meanwhile, my teacher had to go to his native town in U. P. (India) and he asked my mother to send me along so that I complete my studies. This was to ensure my admission into the most trusted institution of religious education in India.

My mother prepared me for my journey but I needed fifty rupees for my travel expenses which she couldn't afford. So she borrowed from someone. In six months, I completed my primary education for my admission the next year. I was enrolled and I started my studies.

I was so engrossed in my studies that I became unconscious of my health, as a result of which I developed tuberculosis. My eyes became very sore. My mother admitted me into Bombay hospital (now Mumbai) and began crying upon seeing my state. When the doctors diagnosed that the disease reached the third stage, they informed us that the chances of my survival was slim. Although they prescribed some medicines for me, they became hopeless. I informed my mother that if I was to die, then why not in the cause of Allāh ﷻ? This made her weep even more. So I continued with my studies in Bombay and spent four months in Jamā'at (In Allāh's path).

I got married and had children. My mother continued sitting with me to listen to the Glorious Qur'ān from me. When Hellfire was mentioned, she would cry but when Paradise was mentioned, she became happy. If I ever omitted the verses of Hellfire, she would instantly notice it and remind me to recite it.

The final year of my studies was the most distressful moment for me. My mother lost her eyesight and all of her teeth due to extreme old age. Her legs weakened and could no longer walk, but still she sent me fifteen hundred miles away to complete my studies.

I was unaware that her condition deteriorated even further upon my arrival at the Madrasah. All the relatives were informed of her severe illness. Most of the relatives including my sisters gathered. They suggested to send a telegram to me but she refused and said , "If I die and Allāh ﷻ asks: What have you brought? I shall say, "My Lord, I am empty handed but have left behind my son in Your path. My son will serve the cause of my pardoning."

A state of drowsiness overcame her. My sisters and others washed her and changed her clothes. When she was laid on her bed, she explained the sweet fragrance surrounding her.

Thereupon she said, "As Salāmu Alaikum Wa Rahmatullāhi Wa Barakātuhu" (May peace, mercy and the blessings of Allāh ﷻ be upon you). She laughed and then instantly became unconscious.

When she recovered, the women around asked why she laughed and whom did she greet. She told them that she saw her son (Umar Pālanpūri) coming between two angels, so she greeted the angels and smiled when she saw me.

Just imagine, she had lost her eyesight and could not see the people around her yet saw her son who was fifteen hundred miles away. Later I was informed that she passed away.

All of her prayers, upbringing of her children, efforts, sacrifices and her Du'ās for her son, came to be apparent as a result of which, Muslims in their thousands benefitted from Shaykh Umar Pālanpūri ﷺ. He became a Muballigh (orator) of Tablīgh, who not only gave speeches to the masses but even spoke in the gatherings of scholars of the Arab world.

Mother of Mufti Taqi Uthmāni

Mufti Taqi Uthmāni writes: The biggest support to me and hope of life, after my father's death was my mother. Despite being bed-ridden and grief stricken, her presence was a source of encouragement for us all. Her affection would remove all of our worries and her kind words would free us from all bitterness of life. Now she has passed on, she took with her the peace, comfort and serenity of the home.

Man is ungrateful by nature and the real value of any person or thing can only be known when it is gone. When I think of my mother, I think to myself of how a great gift she was from Allāh ﷻ. Those whose mothers are still alive, are very fortunate. Casting a look of love on her face brings rewards equal to that of performing Hajj. Uwais Qarni's place became enviable for the Companions of the Holy Prophet ﷺ, though he did not see the Holy Prophet ﷺ because of his service towards his mother. She is never appreciated when she is alive but after death, regretting is of no use. He granted me the opportunity to serve my mother for thirty years and now, my mother has journeyed to the afterlife forever and her vacant room reminds me of the carelessness on my part of service towards her.

I feel that my efforts to take care of her were nothing compared to her great favours. All mothers are kind and affectionate to their children. As well as being a mother, she was also a teacher. She educated us all not with books or lectures, but through practice. Her life represented a complete code of noble precepts and practices.

I learned so much through her contentment, untiring efforts, sacrifice, self-respect and courage. My father's entire life was devoted to the cause of Islām and my mother supported him in all conditions and circumstances. She relieved him from all domestic worries to let him continue with his Dīni service. I always hope that her contribution to my father's well-being shall be highly regarded in the Hereafter. She gave Bai'ah to Shaykh Ashraf Ali Thānwi ﷺ. She had great longing for worship. The recitation of the Holy Qur'ān, constant Dhikr of Allāh ﷻ and praying the Nawāfil (optional prayers) until after midnight in addition to the prescribed prayers was her daily practice. She continued all that with full enthusiasm until her long illness confined her to her bed.

She would be extremely busy with the house work, looking after the children, fulfilling her responsibilities towards my father, tending to her sick and aged mother-in-law, from early morning to late night. Allāh ﷻ bestowed His great blessing upon her. She performed Hajj twice and Umrah once. She remained bed ridden for the last thirteen years of her life and continued her practice of prayers as long as she could. But she was unable to do it after suffering a major stroke that left her permanently disabled. She would turn her face in the direction of the Ka'bah and murmur the words of prayer. It was Saturday, 20th Rajab when she, out of intense thirst, drank water in excess, which caused flatulence in her stomach. Meanwhile, there was Adhān for the night prayer and in the struggle to turn towards the Ka'bah, she fainted. My elder brother Muhammad Radi, in whose house she resided, tried to support her but found her suffering from another stroke. She began vomiting and ceased to speak.

We were surprised when suddenly her hands started moving under the pillow in search for something. I realised that she was searching for her rosary (Tasbīh beads) to recite, as she would keep it under her pillow. She took her beads for a while but then fell unconscious again. The last movement of her body in her senses was to perform Salāh and of the hands to count the Tasbīh.

She was transferred to the Defence Medical Centre on the advice of the doctors where she was given the best possible treatment, but her end was nearing. She was in a coma from Monday to Thursday, until 4pm , her breathing became irregular, which indicated the red signal. The doctors tried till the last moment while I recited Sūrah Yāsīn at her head side. The last words of the Sūrah were on the tongue when she breathed her last. It was the month of Rajab, when my dear mother went to meet her Creator. Her face was calm and relaxed after years of distress and tension. Shaykh Dr. Abdul Hayy Ārifi ﷺ led the funeral prayer and she was buried close to my father's grave. May Allāh ﷻ shower His Infinite Mercy upon her, forgive her and elevate her station in Paradise, Āmīn.

Share Your Time

A man came home from work late again, tired and irritated, to find his five year old son waiting for him at the door. "Daddy, may I ask you a question?"

"Yeah, sure, what is it ?" replied the father. "Daddy, how much money do you make an hour?"

"That's none of your business! What makes you ask such a thing?" the father said angrily. "I just want to know. Please tell me, how much do you make an hour ?" pleaded the little boy. "If you must know I make £20 an hour."

"Oh," the little boy replied, head bowed. Looking up, he said, "Daddy may I borrow £10?"

The father was furious, "If the only reason you wanted to know how much money I make, is just so you can borrow some to buy a silly toy or some other nonsense, then you march yourself straight to your room and go to bed. Think about why you're being so selfish. I work long hard hours everyday and don't have time for such childish games."

The little boy quietly went to his room and shut the door. The man sat down and started to get even more angry about the little boy's questioning. How dare he ask such questions only to get some money.

After an hour or so, the man had calmed down, and started to think he may have been a little hard on his son. Maybe there was something he really needed to buy with that £10, and he really didn't ask for money very often. The man went to the door of the little boy's room and opened the door. "Are you sleeping son?" he asked. "No daddy, I am awake," replied the boy. "I've been thinking, maybe I was too hard on you earlier," said the father. "It's been a long day and I took my aggravation out on you. Here is that £10 you asked for."

The little boy sat straight up, beaming. "Oh, thank you daddy!" he yelled. Then, reaching under his pillow he pulled out some more crumpled up notes. The father, seeing that the boy already had money, started getting angry again. The little boy slowly counted out his money, then looked up at the father. "Why did you want more money if you already had some!" the father grumbled.

"Because I didn't have enough, but now I do," the little boy replied. "Daddy, I have £20 now. Can I buy an hour of your time?"

Share some time with those who need you. They need your time more than you will ever know!

Information Please

When I was young, my father had one of the first telephones in our neighbourhood. I remember it well, the polished old case fastened to the wall. The shiny receiver hung on the side of the box. I was too little to reach the telephone, but I used to listen with fascination when my mother used to talk through it.

Then I discovered that somewhere inside this wonderful device lived an amazing person – her name was "Information Please" and there was nothing she did not know. "Information Please" could supply anybody's number and the correct time.

My first personal experience with this anonymous individual came when one day, my mother was visiting a neighbour. Amusing myself at the tool bench in the basement, I hit my finger with a hammer. The pain was terrible, but there didn't seem to be any reason in crying because there was no one home to sympathise with me.

I walked around the house sucking my throbbing finger, finally arriving at the stairway. The telephone! Quickly, I ran for the footstool in the room and dragged it to the landing. Climbing up, I unhooked the receiver in the hall and held it to my ear.

"Information Please," I said into the mouthpiece just above my head. A click or two and a small clear voice spoke into my ear. "Information....I hurt my finger..." I wailed into the phone. The tears came readily enough now that I had an audience.

"Isn't your mother home?" came the question. "Nobody's home but me," I blubbered. She asked, "Are you bleeding?" "No," I replied. "I hit my finger with the hammer and it hurts." "Can you open your icebox?" she asked. I said I could. "Then chip off a little piece of ice and hold it to your finger said the voice.

After that, I called "Information Please" for everything. I asked her for help with my geography and she told me where Philadelphia was. She helped me with my Maths. Then, there was the time, our pet canary died. I called "Information Please" and told her the sad story. She listened, and then said the usual thing grown-ups say to soothe a child. But I was un-consoled. I asked her, "Why is it that birds should sing so beautifully and bring joy to all families, only to end up as a heap of feathers on the bottom of a cage?"

She must have sensed my deep concern, for she said quietly, "Always remember that there are other worlds they sing in." Somehow I felt better. Another day I was on the telephone. "Information Please".....""Information! How do you spell fix?" I asked.

All this took place in a small town in the Pacific Northwest. When I was nine years old, we moved across the country to live in Boston. I missed my friend very much. "Information Please," belonged in that old wooden box back home, and I somehow never thought of trying the tall, shiny new phone that sat on the table in the hall.

As I grew into my teens, the old memories of my childhood conversations never really left me. Often, in moments of doubt and perplexity, I would recall the serene sense of security I had. I appreciated now, how patient, understanding and kind she was to have spent her time talking to a little boy.

A few years later, on my way West, to college, my plane landed in Seattle. I had about half an hour or so between places. I spent 15 minutes or so on the phone with my sister, who lived there. Then, without thinking what I was doing, I dialled my hometown operator and said, "Information Please." Miraculously, I heard the small, clear voice I knew so well, "Information."

I hadn't planned this but I heard myself saying, "Could you please tell me how to spell fix?" There was a long pause. Then, came the soft spoken answer, "I guess your finger must have healed by now." I laughed. "So, it's really still you," I said. "I wonder if you have any idea how much you meant to me during that time."

"I wonder," she said, "If you knew how much your calls meant to me. I never had any children and I used to look forward to your calls."

I told her how often I had thought of her over the years and asked if I could call her again when I come back to visit my sister. "Please do!" she said. "Just ask for Sārah."

Three months later I was back in Seattle. A different voice answered "Information." I asked for Sārah. "Are you a friend?" she asked. "Yes, a very old friend," I answered.

"I'm sorry to have to tell you this," she said. "Sārah had been working part-time the last few years because she was sick. She died five weeks ago." Before I could hang up she said, "Wait a minute. Did you say your name was Ādam?" "Yes." "Well, Sārah left a message for you. She wrote it down in case you called. Let me read it to you."

The note said, "Tell him, I still say there are other worlds to sing in. He'll know what I mean." I thanked her and hung up. I knew what Sārah meant.

Never underestimate the impression you make on others. Sometimes people come into your life and you know right away that they were meant to be there to serve some sort of purpose, teach you a lesson or help you figure out who you are or what to become. You never know who these people are who can change your life forever.

You know the very moment that they will affect your life in some profound way. Sometimes things happen to you at a time that may seem horrible, painful and unfair, but in reflection you realise that without overcoming these obstacles, you would have never realised your potential, strength and willpower.

Everything happens for a reason. Nothing happens by chance or by means of good luck. Illness, injury, love, lost moments of true greatness and sheer stupidity all occur to test the limits of your being. Without these small tests, life would be like a smoothly paved, straight flat road to nowhere. It would be safe and comfortable, but dull and utterly pointless.

The people you meet in your life affect you one way or another . The successes and downfalls you experience build you into becoming something and the bad experiences teach you things for life. In fact, they are probably the most emotional and important ones.

If someone hurts you, betrays you or breaks your heart, forgive them because they have helped you learn about trust and the importance of being cautious to whomever you open your heart. Talk to people you have never talked to before, listen to them and have the willingness to learn always.

If someone loves you, love them back unconditionally not just because they love you but because they are teaching you to love and to open your heart and eyes to little things. Make every day count. Appreciate every moment and take from it everything that you possibly can, for you may never be able to experience it again.

Orphans with Parents

Mūsa and Fātimah, two bubbly and vibrant five year old twins, try to draw their parent's attention to the lovely sandcastles they had been constructing for hours in the garden. Dad is too busy viewing television and replying to emails on his Blackberry, while mum has for the last few hours, been chatting with her friends and updating her Facebook status. Mum and Dad hardly take notice of their kid's achievement. Both parents are usually so involved in their work and social environments that they "hardly" spend time with their kids.

Apart from the first four months spent with mum, after birth, both Mūsa and Fātimah have ever since infancy been inhabitants of a day care centre. In the evenings, mum picks them up on her way back home from the office. Dad usually returns late in the evening and both parents barely have time to interact with their kids before its time to sleep and wake-up again.

This is a strange phenomenon of children with both parents but are "modern day orphans".

Due to many parents' deep engrossment in the material and social environment, they are unable to spend basic and vital time with their children, thus, neglecting them and reducing them to the level of 'modern day orphans'. Parents are there, but in reality they are not there.

Child neglect is a very common type of child abuse. It is a regular failure to adequately provide the child with its basic needs. it relates not only to food, education and clothing, but also lack of emotional and spiritual support, hygiene and supervision. Child neglect is not always easy to spot but parents are often oblivious of this syndrome.

Recently, a teacher from a primary school asked her students to write an essay about what they would like for themselves....

Whilst marking the essays, she read one that made her very emotional. Her husband had just walked in, saw her crying and asked her, "What happened?"

She answered, "Read this. It's one of my student's essays." It read as follows. "O' Allāh ﷻ, tonight I ask you something very special: Make me into a television. I want to take its place. Live like the TV in my house. Have my own special place and have my family around ME. To be taken seriously when I talk... I want to be the centre of attention and be heard without interruptions or questions. I want to receive the same special care that the TV receives when it is not working. I want the company of my Dad when he arrives home from work tired and I want my Mum to want me when she is sad and upset, instead of ignoring me... and... I want my brothers to fight to be with me. I want to feel that family just leaves everything aside, every now and then, just to spend some time with me. Last but not least, make it that I can make them all happy and entertain them... Allāh ﷻ, I don't ask you for much... I just want to live like every TV".

At that moment, the husband said, "By Allāh ﷻ, poor child. What horrible parents!" She looked up at him and said, "The writer of this essay is our son!"

Makes you think doesn't it? The significance of child neglect should come to no surprise, given the present day lack of parental care and nurturance. It is so crucial to offer our children care in terms of educational training, emotional support and spiritual guidance. The heart of a child must be filled with love and Imān. A child's mind must be entertained with proper guidance, knowledge and wisdom and not left to be nurtured by peer pressure, social networking and immoral television programs. Allāh ﷻ says,

$$ يَا أَيُّهَا الَّذِيْنَ آمَنُوا قُوا أَنْفُسَكُمْ وَأَهْلِيْكُمْ نَارًا $$

"O those who believe! Save yourselves and your families from the Fire." (66:6)

The Noble Messenger of Allāh ﷺ said: "Every one of you is a shepherd and is questionable about his flock. The leader of people is a guardian and is questionable about his subjects. A man is the guardian of his family and he is questionable about them. A woman is the guardian of her husband's home and his children and she is questionable about them. The servant of a man is a guardian of the property of his master and he is questionable about it. Nay! Every one of you is a shepherd and is questionable about his flock."

(Bukhāri, Muslim)

One of the greatest titles in the world is 'parent' and one of the biggest blessings in the world is to have caring and loving parents to call mum and dad. There is no friendship and no love like that of the parent for the child. Have fun with your kids, laugh with them and talk to them. Children remember having fun more than they remember having things. When they are older, they look back and remember fun things you did together, not the expensive PlayStations, IPads, mobiles or toys you gave them.

The Messenger of Allāh ﷺ was casual and loving towards children. He once kissed his grandchild while a Companion witnessed this action and said; "I have ten children and have never kissed one of them." The Messenger of Allāh ﷺ cast a look at him and said, "Whoever is not merciful to others will not be treated mercifully."

(Bukhāri)

Children are a great boon both in this world and in the Hereafter as the Noble Messenger of Allāh ﷺ in this context, said, "When someone dies, their deeds (righteous acts) come to an end, apart from three: Sadaqah Jāriyah (ongoing charity), beneficial knowledge or a pious child who prays for them (the deceased).   (Muslim)

So never orphan your children by neglecting them even when you are still around. Children are very much in need of love and care and in return, they will love and care for you in times when you need it the most!

A Parent/Child Relationship

Scene 1:
Construction of the Ka'bah, an old father Ibrāhīm ﷺ and his young son working together to raise the walls of Ka'bah.

Scene 2:
Session in court, father Dāwūd ﷺ and son Sulaimān ﷺ sitting together trying to solve the problem together. Son came up with a solution; father embraces it because there is no competition between the two. They both wanted to reach a conclusion together.

Scene 3:
Son Yūsuf ﷺ saw a dream, he shares it with his father before anyone else. Father listens to it carefully and guides his son about the interpretation of the dream.

Scene 4:
Father Ibrāhīm ﷺ saw a dream, shares it with his son directly. Son takes it so positively and advices his father to act upon it.

Scene 5:
Mother puts her son Mūsā ﷺ in a case, slides him into a river then transfers the whole mission to her daughter. Daughter handles it so well that she took care of it. Mother trusted her daughter completely and daughter didn't let her mother down.

Scene 6:
Father Luqmān gave beautiful advice to his son with understanding, love and Hikmah. Son listens to his advice seriously.

Today we have this dilemma called: "Generation Gap." How can we bridge this gap? How can we have the same type of relationship as we see in the Qur'ān?

The answer:
The common themes in all of the scenes above are:
1. Understanding
2. Trust in the relationship
3. Common goals
4. Caring and respectful attitude
5. Communication
6. Same level of understanding of Dīn
7. They read the same Book
8. They share the same interest; to serve Allāh ﷻ

This can happen if we connect ourselves and our children to the Book of Allāh ﷻ, Inshā-Allāh.

Imagine!
Mother and daughter come home after a class and discuss what they have learnt together.
Imagine!
Father and son discussing together how to solve a problem in a local Masjid.

Imagine!
The whole family is on the same page when it comes to Dīn. May Allāh ﷻ make our families support and assist us in Dīn. Āmīn.

Daughters are Special

A daughter is not equal to tension, but in today's world, a daughter is equal to ten sons.

A father asked his daughter: Who would you love more, me or your husband?
The best reply given by the daughter: I don't know really, but when I see you, I forget him, but when I see him, I remember you.

You can always call your daughter as beyta (son), but you can never call your son as beyti (daughter).

That's why daughters are very special.

The Soldier

"Mum and Dad, I'm coming home, but I have a favour to ask. I have a friend I'd like to bring home with me." "Sure," they replied. "We'd love to meet him."

"There's something you should know," the son continued. "He was hurt pretty badly in the battle. He stepped on a land mine and lost an arm and a leg. He has nowhere else to go and I want him to come and live with us."

"I'm sorry to hear that son. Maybe we can help him find somewhere to live." "No, Mum and Dad, I want him to live with us." "Son," said the father. "You don't know what you're asking. Someone with such a handicap would be a terrible burden on us. We have our own lives to live and we can't let something like this interfere with our lives. I think you should just come home and forget about this person. He'll find a way to live on his own."

At that point, the son hung up on the phone. The parents heard nothing more from him. A few days later, however, they received a call from the San Francisco police. Their son had died after falling from a building, they were told. The police believed it was suicide. The grief-stricken parents flew to San Francisco and were taken to the city morgue to identify the body of their son. They recognized him, but to their horror they also discovered something they didn't know, their son had only one arm and one leg.

The parents in this story leave a lesson for all of us. We find it easy to love those who are good-looking or fun to have around, but we don't like people who inconvenience us or make us feel uncomfortable. We would rather stay away from people who aren't as healthy, beautiful or smart as we are.

We need to supplicate to Allāh ﷻ that He gives us the strength that we need to accept people as they are, and to help us all be more understanding of those who are different from us!

Spending on One's Family on Āshūra Day

Rasūlullāh ﷺ is authentically reported to have said: "Whoever expands his spending on his family on the day of Āshūra, Allāh ﷻ will inflate his sustenance for the rest of that year."

(Shu'abul Imān and Al-Istidhkār)

It has been tried and tested as several narrators of this Hadīth have echoed the following testimony, "We have tried this and have found it to be accurate." (Al-Istidhkār)

In fact, one narrator of this Hadīth, a great Muhaddith and Faqīh, Sufyān Ibn 'Uyaynah ﷺ said, "I have been doing this for fifty to sixty years and have always seen its benefit." (Latīful Ma'ārif)

Spend generously on your family, especially on this special day and receive the reward Allāh ﷻ has promised.

The Holiday Season

Coping with Emotionally Draining Family Get-togethers

On contemplating upon the emphasis placed on maintaining family ties in Islām, one could easily conclude it does not come naturally. Indeed, difficult and dysfunctional family members can make the holiday season excruciating to bear, at the least, capped with tons of patience. As many guidelines and rewards as there are in the Sunnah with regards to patience, tolerance, respecting the elders, honouring parents etc., even the most willing is tested by guests and visiting family. On the virtue of visiting and spending time together, Allāh ﷻ has honoured this duty.

"A man visited a brother of his in a village. Allāh ﷻ dispatched an angel to wait for him on the road. The angel asked, 'Where are you going?' He replied, 'To a brother of mine in this village.' He said, 'Is he responsible for some blessing you have?' He said, 'No, I love him for Allāh ﷻ.' He said, 'I am a messenger of Allāh ﷻ to you. Allāh ﷻ loves you as you love him." (Al-Adabul Mufrad).

Our beloved Prophet ﷺ did however teach us principles that stands true to the test of time regarding guests:

$$زُرْ غِبًّا تَزْدَدْ حُبًّا$$

"Visit each other (for short visits) sometimes and love will increase." (Tabarāni, Baihaqi)

Guests should not willingly outstay their limited time but be mindful of their words and their points for conversation and be aware of tacit boundaries. Most importantly, they must be mindful of the parameters of Hijāb, making it easy for females to feel comfortable and welcomed even if they wear Niqāb.

With regards to spite, nastiness and malice, we can take pointers from Dr Karen Ruskin:

1. Choose to be the side of yourself that you want to be, not the side of you that is in negative reactive response mode to another's behaviour.
This is the side of yourself that feels comfortable to you and makes you feel in control rather than reactive to someone's comments about you.

2. What someone else says or does, says something about them and nothing about you
Your nit-picky aunt tells you, "Looks like you gained some weight since I have seen you last." Tell yourself, "It is my aunt's insecurities about her own weight that leads her to notice another's weight."

3. Have your spouse's back.
How we communicate not only directly to our spouses, but what we say and do not say about them to family is of huge significance. For instance, if your wife is already uptight, predicting that your mother is going to say something mean because that is the typical pattern,

choose to have your wife's back in a polite way to your mother. "Mum, I love you dearly, those were hurtful words you said to my wife, of whom you know I love deeply. Please! This is a gift that we can all be together so let's cherish it."

4. Hear Our Children's Voices.
A child who feels their voice matters, even in what is being unsaid, will treat themselves and others respectfully.

5. Raise real concerns and issues
When there are arguments and fights among parents, siblings and our extended families, you should try to raise real concerns and issues:

a. Ask, 'What are we really fighting about?' Does your daughter/son/son-in-law etc. feel disrespected? Is mum mad that you never call? Discuss what is really wrong.

b. Examine your contribution to the problem. Are you passive or aggressive? Overreacting? Passing blame? Accept responsibility.

c. Explain your anger, don't show it, better yet, leave it at the door. You can pick it up on the way out.

d. Find something fun and mutually satisfying to do together instead of the negative pattern. Baking? Hiking? Couples who try new activities together are happier. It can be true of mums and daughters, fathers and sons and adult siblings too.

Finally, some Sunnah guidelines:

Avoid suspicion & think positive of others.
"Be careful of suspicion, for it is the most mistaken of all speech. Do not spy on others, nor compete among yourselves, do not envy one another or despise one another. Rather, be servants of Allāh ﷻ and brothers." (Bukhāri)

Give gifts to each other.
"Give gifts to one another and you will love one another." (Bukhāri)

Have a sense of shame.
Among the well-known wisdom of the Prophet ﷺ is the saying, "If you have no shame, then do as you please." (Bukhāri)

Do not look for faults in others.
"A believer is not a fault-finder, abusive, obscene, nor harsh." (Bukhāri)

Pray for good character.

اَللّٰهُمَّ إِنِّي أَعُوذُ بِكَ مِنْ مُنْكَرَاتِ الْأَخْلَاقِ، وَالْأَعْمَالِ وَالْأَهْوَاءِ

"O Allāh! I seek refuge in You from undesirable manners, deeds and aspirations." (Tirmizi)

We ask Allāh ﷻ for Tawfīq. Āmīn!

Speeding Ticket

Zubair took a long look at his speedometer before slowing down from 73mph in a 55mph zone. Fourth time in as many months, how could a person get caught so often? When his car had slowed to 10mph, Zubair pulled over, but only partially. Let the police worry about the potential traffic hazard.

The policeman was stepping out of his car, with the big pad in hand. "Shu'ayb? Shu'ayb from the Holy Qur'ān Halqa group? The same Halqa group of about 60 students who attend every Wednesdays at Shaykh Shākir's home. Zubair sunk further into his trench coat. This was worse than the coming ticket. A policeman catching a guy from his own Halqa group.

A guy who happened to be a little eager to get home after a long day at the office. Jumping out of the car, he approached a man he saw every Wednesday, a man he'd never seen in uniform. "Shu'ayb, I didn't fancy meeting you like this". "Guess you caught me red-handed in a rush to see my wife and kids," he said.

"Yes, I guess." Zubair seemed uncertain. "I've seen some long days at the office lately. I'm afraid I bent the rules a bit, just this once." Zubair toed at a pebble on the pavement. "Rāzia said something about roast and potatoes tonight. You know what I mean?" "I know what you mean. I also know that you have a reputation in our precinct." Ouch. This was not going in the right direction. It was time to change tactics.

"What did you clock me at?" "Seventy," he said. Would you sit back in your car please?" "Now, wait a minute, Shu'ayb. I checked as soon as I saw you, I was barely nudging 65." The lie seemed to come easier with every ticket. "Please, Zubair, in the car."

Flustered, Zubair hunched himself through the still-open door. Slamming it shut, he stared at the dashboard. He was in no rush to open the window. The minutes ticked by.

Shu'ayb scribbled away on the pad. Why hadn't he asked for a driver's license? Whatever the reason, it would be a week before Zubair ever sat near this cop again at the Halqa.

A tap on the door jerked his head to the left. There was Shu'ayb, a folded paper in hand. Zubair rolled down the window a mere two inches, just enough room for Shu'ayb to pass him the slip. "Thanks."

Zubair could not quite keep the sneer out of his voice. Shu'ayb returned to his police car without a word. Zubair watched his retreat in the mirror. Zubair unfolded the sheet of paper. How much was this one going to cost? Wait a minute. What was this? Some kind of joke? Certainly not a ticket?

Zubair began to read, "Dear Zubair, Once, I had a daughter. She was six when she was killed by a car. You guessed it, a speeding driver. A fine and three months in jail and the man was free. Free to hug his daughters. All three of them. I only had one and I'm never going to hug her again. A thousand times, I've tried to forgive that man. A thousand times I thought I had. Maybe I did, but I need to do it again. Even now pray for me and be careful. Zubair, my son, is all I have left." – Shu'ayb.

Zubair turned around in time to see Shu'ayb's car pull away and head down the road. Zubair watched until it disappeared. A full 15 minutes later, he too, pulled away and drove home slowly, praying for forgiveness and hugging a surprised wife and kids when he arrived.

"A lesson in speeding, he will never forget!"

Desire of an Old Woman and Her Husband

An old woman and her husband use to earn their living together as woodcutters collecting two bundles of wood and cutting them every day. They sold one bundle in the market and kept the other to warm themselves. Despite their poor living condition they expected to get a little more richer that year. However, they would constantly complain bitterly about their fate.

One day on their way to the forest, by chance they met a saintly person, which was a rare luck for them. This saintly person offered them a choice, "In my left hand there is a treasure, so you can pay for whatever you desire and in my right hand, there is abstinence - moderation of desire."

Realising that such an opportunity came only once in a lifetime, the husband chose the left hand without any hesitation and as for abstinence which they practised for many years, is of no longer concern now.

Because of the money, the wife wished to have tastier food. Each evening for a year they would spend on exquisite cuisine. But very soon, realised that they could never serve themselves with all the existing dishes, so they gave up.

Thereafter, they thought of repairing their house. The husband remarked, "Why should we suffice with one room when we can afford to pay for a beautiful house?" They called all the best architects in the region and assigned each of them to a specific role, providing them the tools, plans and material, being spoilt with choices, they could not make the right choice.

Wanting to spend their money, they recalled that they wanted to have their own bull. "Why only one?" asked the husband. "We can buy an entire flock." But, the breeds of cattle were numerous, and the couple could not decide which one of the breeds or cross-breeds were the best.

The life of the two old people became very difficult. Every new desire effaces the older and ended up following their desires without gaining any contentment.

At that time the saintly person re-appeared before them, and told them, "You fools! You already had abstinence (and contentment). Where then was the necessity to go after the treasures?"

Moral to be learnt

Knowing how to control one's desires is the greatest knowledge one can ever ask for. By nature, desires are never satisfied. It is better to be satisfied with a little than to always desire more that makes one negligent, eventually not obtaining anything. Enabling to control your desires will help you to teach your children the same.

Contentment upon a little is the key to happiness. Teach your children this. Nafs (desires and ego) is never satisfied and always yearns for more but never brings happiness. The Nafs' desires are like drug addiction. First one starts with one dose, then two, then three, then four, then five, then six, and on and on. At first, one takes the drug once a week, then twice a week, then every day. There is no end to it.

Allāh ﷻ says, "The heart finds peace only with Allāh's ﷻ Dhikr (remembrance)."

This remembrance of Allāh ﷻ in our daily activities and actions is the prescription for peace and contentment and a check against the Nafs (desires).

Take Action Now

Ibnul Qayyim ﷫ said, A girl died in a plague and her father saw her in his dream. He said, "My daughter, tell me about the Hereafter." So she said, 'We've approached a serious matter. We used to know but we didn't act. I swear by Allāh ﷻ, to add one Tasbīh (saying Subhān-Allāh) or a single Rak'āh to my book of deeds is more beloved to me than the whole world and everything in it.

This girl said words of great importance. 'We used to know but we didn't act', but unfortunately most of us don't appreciate this.

We used to know, that if we say Subhān-Allāh Wa Bi Hamdihī 100 times our sins are forgiven even if they're like the foam of the sea. Yet, days and nights pass and we don't say it.

We used to know that two Rak'āt of Duhā prayer is equivalent of paying Sadaqah for 360 joints in our body. Yet, days pass and we do not pray it.

We used to know that fasting a day voluntarily for the sake of Allāh ﷻ distances our face from the fire the distance travelled in 70 years, and we haven't fasted a single day of the week. We used to know that whoever visits a sick person is followed by 70,000 Angels seeking Allāh's ﷻ forgiveness on his behalf but we haven't visited a sick person this week.

We used to know that whoever prayed a funeral prayer and followed it till it was buried has two Qīrāts of reward and a Qīrāt is like the mountain of Uhud, yet weeks pass and we haven't been to the graveyard.

We used to know that whoever builds a Masjid even if it's like a bird's nest, Allāh ﷻ builds a house for them in Paradise. Yet, we haven't contributed to the building of a Masjid, even with ten pounds.

We used to know that the one who supports the widow and her children is like the fighter in the path of Allāh ﷻ and the one who fasts all day and prays all night without sleeping. Yet, we haven't contributed to sponsoring a widow and her children.

We used to know that whoever reads a single letter from the Holy Qur'ān has a good deed and every deed is multiplied ten times. Yet we fail to read it every day.

We used to know that an accepted Hajj has the reward of Jannah and the person returns like the day his mother gave birth to him with a clean book of deeds. However, we haven't performed the rites of Hajj despite our circumstances being made easy for us.

We knew the honour of a believer is in Qiyāmul-Layl (Night Prayers), and that the Prophet ﷺ and His Companions ﷺ never missed it all their lives despite being busy with making a living and fighting in the path of Allāh ﷻ and spreading the religion. But we have neglected this matter terribly.

We knew the Day of Judgement was coming without a doubt and that Allāh ﷻ will resurrect us from our graves, but we haven't prepared for that day.

We used to bury the deceased and pray over them but haven't prepared ourselves for a day like this one, not realising that one day others will bury us.

We know that every breath we take is getting us closer to death, yet we are still busy with amusement and playing. It is time we change the way we're living and prepare properly for the Day of Accounting.

يَوْمَ يَفِرُّ الْمَرْءُ مِنْ أَخِيْهِ . وَأُمِّهِ وَأَبِيْهِ . وَصَاحِبَتِهِ وَبَنِيْهِ . لِكُلِّ امْرِئٍ مِّنْهُمْ يَوْمَئِذٍ شَأْنٌ يُّغْنِيْهِ

"On the Day, a man will flee from his brother, his mother, his father, his wife and his children. For every man that Day will be a matter adequate for him." (80:34-37)

Verily! reminders benefit the Believers.

How to Acquire Barakah in our Lives

The Result of Barakah

If Barakah is found in wealth, it will be spent in the correct avenues such as spending on Masājid, Madrasahs, on the widows, orphans, etc. Spending one's wealth in such causes is actually depositing into one's personal account for investment in the Ākhirah, which he will enjoy in the next world. At the same time, Allāh ﷻ will protect his wealth in this world from unlawful spending.

On the other hand, wealth that is spent on holidays and weekend breaks, etc. is void of Barakah. Generally, such people are short of funds by the middle of the month. Nowadays, we buy things that we don't need, with money that we don't have (bank loans), to impress people that we don't like.

71

Unfortunately, we squander money on special functions such as Nikāh. Rasūlullāh ﷺ is reported to have said, "Verily, the Nikāh with the greatest Barakah (blessings) is the one in which the least expenses are incurred."

This can be understood by a simple example, a scale with two pans; one heavy and one light, the light side rises whilst the heavy side drops. Similarly, the more unnecessary money spent on wedding occasions, the less the blessings. On the other hand, if a simple Nikāh conducted in the Masjid accompanied with the payment of Mahr and followed by a small Walīmah, all in which the least expenses is incurred brings about great blessings. Such simple Nikāh leads to eternal happiness between the spouses as opposed to only short term happiness only.

Factors that contribute towards acquiring blessings in one's life:

1. Earning Halāl sustenance is a means of acquiring an abundance of Barakah in one's life.

2. Performance of our five daily Salāh with Jamā'at in the Masjid.

3. Abstention from unlawful income. A true Muslim does not consume interest or earn unlawful salary.

4. Giving in charity such as Zakāt and Lillāh.

5. To make Salām and Dhikr. One Sahābi complained to Rasūlullāh ﷺ that he is experiencing financial constraint. Rasūlullāh ﷺ said, "On entering your home, make Salām to the inmates of the home loudly and cheerfully. Thereafter, recite Sūrah Ikhlās followed by Durūd Sharīf." The Sahābi says, "By acting on this advice, I was blessed with so much wealth in a short while that I was able to spend on my family and neighbours."

6. Recitation of the Holy Qur'ān within our homes is a source of great blessings and Barakah. For a start, we should recite a minimum of one page at home and one page at the business.

Unfortunately, many of these aspects are missing in our lives and yet if acted upon, will bring about abundance of blessings. A person that goes out in the path of Allāh ﷻ or spends time in a Khānqah and acquires Taqwa will acquire this Barakah in his life as well.

May Allāh ﷻ grant us the Tawfīq upon acting on these advices. Āmīn! (Shaykh Shāh Abdul Hamīd Is'hāq Sāhib)

Ta'līm and Tarbiyah

Salmān al-Odah was once asked, "How do you get your kids to love Salāh?" He said, "Get them to love you."

Always remember that Tarbiyah is founded upon positive relationship. Tarbiyah is nurturing and educating your child such that he/she can reach their full potential as a human and as a Muslim. It is different than Ta'līm, which refers to fact-based education. We often confuse the two, giving our children Ta'līm when they need Tarbiyah. Ta'līm is teaching our children how to perform prayers, memorizing the Duās and learning the positions. Tarbiyah is the cuddling after the prayer when we ask each other, "What did you ask for in Sajdah?"

Ta'līm is memorizing Ahādīth and verses but Tarbiyah is the dinner-table chitchat where we talk about current events and other issues on our mind. Ta'līm is studying Fiqh but Tarbiyah is the loving conversation we have about an incident that happened at school. Ta'līm is studying the Sīrah by memorizing dates and events or preparing for a quiz bowl but Tarbiyah is snuggling in bed and telling stories of brave heroes of the past.

When we were at Umrah, Ustadh Abū Eesā stressed this point a great deal and it has caused a great shift in my own approach to teaching my children. I had asked him if he suggested a program of study for school-aged children. He responded by saying that he was no expert on education and he would leave that to the experienced teachers to develop such a program. He directed us instead to focus our efforts on building relationships with our children as Tarbiyah.

"Tarbiyah," he explained, "is an emotional, not a physical exercise." He explained that in the Qur'ān, we are taught the Du'ā for the parents as follows: "O Allāh! Show mercy on them, as they nurtured me when I was young." In other words, have mercy on them because they did Tarbiyah for me when I was young. It doesn't say "because they 'allamāni"–because they taught me.

Long after facts have come and gone, what a child will remember are the memories of the cuddling on the couch, laughing at stories and warm relaxation in the glow of a parent's attention and love. This relationship is what builds the person up, not the facts and pieces of knowledge imparted. This does not mean we do not teach them facts and knowledge! Those who follow my work know that I do indeed spend time on this Ta'līm. You need to differentiate between the two, so that you give adequate attention to each one of them.

Most importantly, you must understand that you, O' dear parents, are indispensable. You CANNOT outsource Tarbiyah to someone else. You can send your child to classes and Masjid programs for Ta'līm but this can never replace Tarbiyah. The cuddling on the couch, the lively discussions around the table, the one-to-one chats before bed, these are the things that only a parent can do. These are the things that build the foundation of the Islamic Akhlāq and Ādāb (Manners and etiquettes).

Upbringing of Children

As queens and shepherds of their homes, women of Islām took deep interest in training their children. The mothers put in tremendous effort to impart to their children religious training and make them heirs of great leaders and chiefs. We cite some examples that should serve as a lesson for our mothers of today.

Imām Yazīd Ibn Hārūn Wasti ﵀ (d. 206 AH) held a high rank among the Tabiʿ Tābiʿīn (successors of the successors of the Sahābah ﵁). He recounted his life story as a student, saying, "I was away from my family for many years. In Baghdad, I learnt from a Tābiʿī scholar at Askar. I went to him and requested him to narrate to me a Hadīth. He narrated, Sayyidunā Anas Ibn Mālik ﵁ narrated that the Holy Prophet ﷺ said, "If Allāh ﷻ involves someone in an anxiety then he must show patience. He must again show patience and again show patience."

The Shaykh then said that he would not narrate any other Hadīth. Then I returned to my native land. I reached home at night and did not knock at the door lest I wake up my family. However, I opened the door somehow and went in. My wife was sleeping on the roof and I saw a young man sleeping by her. I decided to strike him with a stone but I suddenly remembered the Hadīth of the Shaykh of Askar, so I ceased. I picked up the stone twice or thrice but then checked myself. Suddenly, my wife woke up. Seeing me, she awakened the young man, saying, "Get up! Meet your father." He greeted me warmly. When I had begun the journey, my wife was pregnant. I then realised the blessing of abiding by the Hadīth."

Provide your Children with a Good Breakfast

Generally, mothers do not give their children a very healthy breakfast. They regard tea and biscuits as an adequate meal. This does no good for the child's health. Such an inadequate meal will make him weak and affect his development. His body will lack the vital vitamins and calcium.

Therefore, an understanding mother with this intention that the child would grow up to be strong and healthy and through this he would spread the message of Dīn to every point on the globe should feed her children a nutritional breakfast. For example, she may feed them with milk, eggs, fruit etc. A famous Persian expression reveals, "A morsel in the morning is better than chicken and fish."

In other words, a little bit of food early in the morning is far better than thousands of other blessings. In our ancient form of medicine, a good breakfast was very strongly recommended because the whole day hinges on breakfast. If a person has a good nutritional breakfast, there would not be a problem even if he has a very light snack for lunch. Therefore, we should feed our children and ourselves as well, according to our ability, with a good, wholesome and nutritional breakfast. Very starchy or oily foods are detrimental to the health. Fried food is harmful particularly to children who have to sit at school all day long. With the children's intense physical training, even these foods may digest rapidly (leaving them hungry again). So avoid these foods for breakfast, prepare a daily breakfast menu that is both appetising as well as nutritious. Whilst preparing your menu, take into account the seasons as well. A half boiled egg is very appetising and beneficial to the health.

Add the juice of a freshly squeezed lemon to water (1/2 a lemon to a glass of water). Feed this juice to your children and you too should drink it.

This is very beneficial to the throat and the eyes. Similarly, carrots are good for the eyesight and it also increases the blood.

Apart from this, the primary ingredient of a good breakfast is cereal. Most homes do not even bother about it. Cereals are full of vitamins. Cereals are a good source of nutrition and their nutritional value is further increased when milk is added. Make cereals a must in your breakfast. The cereals need to be changed from time to time otherwise the child will get fed up eating the same cereal daily.

Important Advice on the Moral & Character Building of the Child

A Hadīth states, "Among the gifts a father gives to his son, none is better than excellent etiquette and good manners." (Tirmizi)

The Holy Prophet ﷺ said, "Treat children with kindness and give them good education." (Ibn Mājah)

It is the right of the children that their father provides them with a good education, gives them a good name and fulfils their duties according to their age and intellectual growth. Train children to be truthful and trustworthy, stable and unselfish, helpful to the distressed, respectful to the elders and guests and polite to neighbours.

Inculcate in Children the Habit of Reading

Children must be encouraged to develop an ability to ponder, to comprehend and to read. They must distinguish between knowledge and ignorance and realise the superiority of an Ālim (scholar) over an ignorant person. Mention the respect, virtues and status of the learned.

When children observe the esteem and high rank enjoyed by the Ulamā (scholars) and men of wisdom, and the deprivation and misfortune of the ignorant, they will be motivated to learn and study earnestly. When the high rewards of an Ālim is witnessed, learning and studying will be valued. Knowledge revives the heart and brightens the soul. It gives strength to the body, fights fear and shows humans the right path. It is a means of attaining high position in this world as well as the next. An Ālim is compassionate and distinguishes between the lawful and unlawful. Knowledge is the lender, action is its follower. It is the destiny of the fortunate. The unfortunate are deprived of it. Knowledge is peculiar to human beings. It was because of knowledge that Sayyidunā Ādam u enjoyed superiority over the angels. It is the duty of humans to put knowledge to use. Hasan Basri ﷺ is known to have said that if it was given a form, knowledge would be more beautiful than the sun, the moon and the stars.

A good way to arouse interest in advance learning is to organise competition for children. These competitions may be for speed reading, the number of books read during a certain period and an examination held on the books studied or read. Children who do well should be rewarded and encouraged. This could also take the form of putting in a good word about them in the presence of other people.

Explain to children that reading for the sake of Allāh ﷻ is an Ibādah. Children should be provided an ideal atmosphere suitable for studies. They must be allowed peace and comfort in a well-lit, clean and ventilated place that protects them from heat and cold. They must have their materials at hand, including religious books. Children should realise that time is like a sword, if you do not cut with it, it will cut you. Duties and responsibilities are important. There is always more to learn, the unknown exceeds the known. Islām calls upon its adherent to put to proper use the time that is available to them. Islām expects us to attain what is beneficial. People must realise the importance of time. Parents must observe the following measures for any programme of study to be successful. Children must:

- Use the knowledge that is obtained to propagate Islām and benefit Muslims.
- Commentate while studying and be attentive fully to what is read and heard. Underline in pencil the main points that one comes across so that it can be easily seen during a second reading. Jot down in the page margins the important issues that are found on that page.
- In a separate notebook, compile an index of the topics of interest.

Other titles from JKN Publications

Your Questions Answered

An outstanding book written by Shaykh Mufti Saiful Islām. A very comprehensive yet simple Fatāwa book and a source of guidance that reaches out to a wider audience i.e. the English speaking Muslims. The reader will benefit from the various answers to questions based on the Laws of Islām relating to the beliefs of Islām, knowledge, Sunnah, pillars of Islām, marriage, divorce and contemporary issues.

UK RRP: £7.50

Hadeeth for Beginners

A concise Hadeeth book with various Ahādeeth that relate to basic Ibādāh and moral etiquettes in Islām accessible to a wider readership. Each Hadeeth has been presented with the Arabic text, its translation and commentary to enlighten the reader, its meaning and application in day-to-day life.

UK RRP: £3.00

Du'ā for Beginners

This book contains basic Du'ās which every Muslim should recite on a daily basis. Highly recommended to young children and adults studying at Islamic schools and Madrasahs so that one may cherish the beautiful treasure of supplications of our beloved Prophet e in one's daily life, which will ultimately bring peace and happiness in both worlds, Inshā-Allāh.

UK RRP: £2.00

How well do you know Islām?

An exciting educational book which contains 300 multiple questions and answers to help you increase your knowledge on Islām! Ideal for the whole family, especially children and adult students to learn new knowledge in an enjoyable way and cherish the treasures of knowledge that you will acquire from this book. A very beneficial tool for educational syllabus.

UK RRP: £3.00

Treasures of the Holy Qur'ān

This book entitled "Treasures of the Holy Qur'ān" has been compiled to create a stronger bond between the Holy Qur'ān and the readers. It mentions the different virtues of Sūrahs and verses from the Holy Qur'ān with the hope that the readers will increase their zeal and enthusiasm to recite and inculcate the teachings of the Holy Qur'ān into their daily lives.

UK RRP: £3.00

Marriage - A Complete Solution
Islām regards marriage as a great act of worship. This book has been designed to provide the fundamental teachings and guidelines of all what relates to the marital life in a simplified English language. It encapsulates in a nutshell all the marriage laws mentioned in many of the main reference books in order to facilitate their understanding and implementation.

UK RRP: £5.00

Pearls of Luqmān
This book is a comprehensive commentary of Sūrah Luqmān, written beautifully by Shaykh Mufti Saiful Islām. It offers the reader with an enquiring mind, abundance of advice, guidance, counselling and wisdom.

The reader will be enlightened by many wonderful topics and anecdotes mentioned in this book, which will create a greater understanding of the Holy Qur'ān and its wisdom. The book highlights some of the wise sayings and words of advice Luqmān u gave to his son.

UK RRP: £3.00

Arabic Grammar for Beginners
This book is a study of Arabic Grammar based on the subject of Nahw (Syntax) in a simplified English format. If a student studies this book thoroughly, he/she will develop a very good foundation in this field, Inshā-Allāh. Many books have been written on this subject in various languages such as Arabic, Persian and Urdu. However, in this day and age there is a growing demand for this subject to be available in English .

UK RRP: £3.00

A Gift to My Youngsters
This treasure filled book, is a collection of Islamic stories, morals and anecdotes from the life of our beloved Prophet e, his Companions y and the pious predecessors. The stories and anecdotes are based on moral and ethical values, which the reader will enjoy sharing with their peers, friends, families and loved ones.

"A Gift to My Youngsters" – is a wonderful gift presented to the readers personally, by the author himself, especially with the youngsters in mind. He has carefully selected stories and anecdotes containing beautiful morals, lessons and valuable knowledge and wisdom.

UK RRP: £5.00

Travel Companion

The beauty of this book is that it enables a person on any journey, small or distant or simply at home, to utilise their spare time to read and benefit from an exciting and vast collection of important and interesting Islamic topics and lessons. Written in simple and easy to read text, this book will immensely benefit both the newly interested person in Islām and the inquiring mind of a student expanding upon their existing knowledge. Inspiring reminders from the Holy Qur'ān and the blessed words of our beloved Prophet e beautifies each topic and will illuminate the heart of the reader. **UK RRP: £5.00**

Pearls of Wisdom

Junaid Baghdādi ﷺ once said, "Allāh ﷻ strengthens through these Islamic stories the hearts of His friends, as proven from the Qur'anic verse,
"And all that We narrate unto you of the stories of the Messengers, so as to strengthen through it your heart." (11:120)
Mālik Ibn Dinār ﷺ stated that such stories are gifts from Paradise. He also emphasised to narrate these stories as much as possible as they are gems and it is possible that an individual might find a truly rare and invaluable gem among them. **UK RRP: £6.00**

Inspirations

This book contains a compilation of selected speeches delivered by Shaykh Mufti Saiful Islām on a variety of topics such as the Holy Qur'ān, Nikāh and eating Halāl. Having previously been compiled in separate booklets, it was decided that the transcripts be gathered together in one book for the benefit of the reader. In addition to this, we have included in this book, further speeches which have not yet been printed.

UK RRP: £6.00

Gift to my Sisters

A thought provoking compilation of very interesting articles including real life stories of pious predecessors, imaginative illustrations and much more. All designed to influence and motivate mothers, sisters, wives and daughters towards an ideal Islamic lifestyle. A lifestyle referred to by our Creator, Allāh ﷻ in the Holy Qur'ān as the means to salvation and ultimate success.

UK RRP: £6.00

Gift to my Brothers

A thought provoking compilation of very interesting articles including real life stories of pious predecessors, imaginative illustrations, medical advices on intoxicants and rehabilitation and much more. All designed to influence and motivate fathers, brothers, husbands and sons towards an ideal Islamic lifestyle. A lifestyle referred to by our Creator, Allāh ﷻ in the Holy Qur'ān as the means to salvation and ultimate success.

UK RRP: £5.00

Heroes of Islām

"In the narratives there is certainly a lesson for people of intelligence (understanding)." (12:111)

A fine blend of Islamic personalities who have been recognised for leaving a lasting mark in the hearts and minds of people.

A distinguishing feature of this book is that the author has selected not only some of the most world and historically famous renowned scholars but also these lesser known and a few who have simply left behind a valuable piece of advice to their nearest and dearest. **UK RRP: £5.00**

Ask a Mufti (3 volumes)

Muslims in every generation have confronted different kinds of challenges. In-spite of that, Islām produced such luminary Ulamā who confronted and re-sponded to the challenges of their time to guide the Ummah to the straight path.

"Ask A Mufti" is a comprehensive three volume fatwa book, based on the Hanafi School, covering a wide range of topics related to every aspect of human life such as belief, ritual worship, life after death and contemporary legal topics related to purity, commercial transaction, marriage, divorce, food, cosmetic, laws pertaining to women, Islamic medical ethics and much more.

UK RRP: £30.00

Should I Follow a Madhab?

Taqleed or following one of the four legal schools is not a new phenomenon. Historically, scholars of great calibre and luminaries, each one being a specialist in his own right, were known to have adhered to one of the four legal schools. It is only in the previous century that a minority group emerged advocating a se-vere ban on following one of the four major schools.

This book endeavours to address the topic of Taqleed and elucidates its im-portance and necessity in this day and age. It will also, by the Divine Will of Allāh ﷻ dispel some of the confusion surrounding this topic. **UK RRP: £5.00**

Advice for the Students of Knowledge

Allāh ﷻ describes divine knowledge in the Holy Qur'ān as a 'Light'. Amongst the qualities of light are purity and guidance. The Holy Prophet ﷺ has clearly ex-plained this concept in many blessed Ahādeeth and has also taught us many supplications in which we ask for beneficial knowledge.

This book is a golden tool for every sincere student of knowledge wishing to mould his/her character and engrain those correct qualities in order to be wor-thy of receiving the great gift of Ilm from Allāh ﷻ. **UK RRP: £3.00**

Stories for Children

"Stories for Children" - is a wonderful gift presented to the readers personally by the author himself, especially with the young children in mind. The stories are based on moral and ethical values, which the reader will enjoy sharing with their peers, friends, families and loved ones. The aim is to present to the children stories and incidents which contain moral lessons, in order to reform and correct their lives, according to the Holy Qur'ān and Sunnah.

UK RRP: £5.00

85

Pearls from My Shaykh

This book contains a collection of pearls and inspirational accounts of the Holy Prophet ﷺ, his noble Companions, pious predecessors and some personal accounts and sayings of our well-known contemporary scholar and spiritual guide, Shaykh Mufti Saiful Islām Sāhib. Each anecdote and narrative of the pious predecessors have been written in the way that was narrated by Mufti Saiful Islām Sāhib in his discourses, drawing the specific lessons he intended from telling the story. The accounts from the life of the Shaykh has been compiled by a particular student based on their own experience and personal observation. **UK RRP: £5.00**

Paradise & Hell

This book is a collection of detailed explanation of Paradise and Hell including the state and conditions of its inhabitants. All the details have been taken from various reliable sources. The purpose of its compilation is for the reader to contemplate and appreciate the innumerable favours, rewards, comfort and unlimited luxuries of Paradise and at the same time take heed from the punishment of Hell. Shaykh Mufti Saiful Islām Sāhib has presented this book in a unique format by including the Tafseer and virtues of Sūrah Ar-Rahmān. **UK RRP: £5.00**

Prayers for Forgiveness

Prayers for Forgiveness' is a short compilation of Du'ās in Arabic with English translation and transliteration. This book can be studied after 'Du'ā for Beginners' or as a separate book. It includes twenty more Du'ās which have not been mentioned in the previous Du'ā book. It also includes a section of Du'ās from the Holy Qur'ān and a section from the Ahādeeth. The book concludes with a section mentioning the Ninety-Nine Names of Allāh ﷻ with its translation and transliteration. **UK RRP: £3.00**

Scattered Pearls

This book is a collection of scattered pearls taken from books, magazines, emails and WhatsApp messages. These pearls will hopefully increase our knowledge, wisdom and make us realise the purpose of life. In this book, Mufti Sāhib has included messages sent to him from scholars, friends and colleagues which will be beneficial and interesting for our readers Inshā-Allāh. **UK RRP: £4.00**

Poems of Wisdom

This book is a collection of poems from those who contributed to the Al-Mumin Magazine in the poems section. The Hadeeth mentions "Indeed some form of poems are full of wisdom." The themes of each poem vary between wittiness, thought provocation, moral lessons, emotional to name but a few. The readers will benefit from this immensely and make them ponder over the outlook of life in general.

UK RRP: £4.00

Horrors of Judgement Day
This book is a detailed and informative commentary of the first three Sūrahs of the last Juz namely; Sūrah Naba, Sūrah Nāzi'āt and Sūrah Abasa. These Sūrahs vividly depict the horrific events and scenes of the Great Day in order to warn mankind the end of this world. These Sūrahs are an essential reminder for us all to instil the fear and concern of the Day of Judgement and to detach ourselves from the worldly pleasures. Reading this book allows us to attain the true realization of this world and provides essential advices of how to gain eternal salvation in the Hereafter.

RRP: £5:00

Spiritual Heart
It is necessary that Muslims always strive to better themselves at all times and to free themselves from the destructive maladies. This book focusses on three main spiritual maladies; pride, anger and evil gazes. It explains its root causes and offers some spiritual cures. Many examples from the lives of the pious predecessors are used for inspiration and encouragement for controlling the above three maladies. It is hoped that the purification process of the heart becomes easy once the underlying roots of the above maladies are clearly understood.   **UK RRP: £5:00**

Hajj & Umrah for Beginners
This book is a step by step guide on Hajj and Umrah for absolute beginners. Many other additional important rulings (Masāil) have been included that will Insha-Allāh prove very useful for our readers. The book also includes some etiquettes of visiting (Ziyārat) of the Holy Prophet's ﷺ blessed Masjid and his Holy Grave.

UK RRP £3:00

Advice for the Spiritual Travellers
This book contains essential guidelines for a spiritual Murīd to gain some familiarity of the science of Tasawwuf. It explains the meaning and aims of Tasawwuf, some understanding around the concept of the soul, and general guidelines for a spiritual Murīd. This is highly recommended book and it is hoped that it gains wider readership among those Murīds who are basically new to the science of Tasawwuf.

UK RRP £3:00

Don't Worry Be Happy
This book is a compilation of sayings and earnest pieces of advice that have been gathered directly from my respected teacher Shaykh Mufti Saiful Islām Sāhib. The book consists of many valuable enlightenments including how to deal with challenges of life, promoting unity, practicing good manners, being optimistic and many other valuable advices. Our respected Shaykh has gathered this Naseehah from meditating, contemplating, analysing and searching for the gems within Qur'anic verses, Ahādeeth and teachings of our Pious Predecessors. **UK RRP £1:00**

Kanzul Bāri

Kanzul Bāri provides a detailed commentary of the Ahādeeth contained in Saheeh al-Bukhāri. The commentary includes Imām Bukhāri's ﷺ biography, the status of his book, spiritual advice, inspirational accounts along with academic discussions related to Fiqh, its application and differences of opinion. Moreover, it answers objections arising in one's mind about certain Ahādeeth. Inquisitive students of Hadeeth will find this commentary a very useful reference book in the final year of their Ālim course for gaining a deeper understanding of the science of Hadeeth.   **UK RRP: £15.00**

How to Become a Friend of Allāh ﷻ

The friends of Allāh ﷻ have been described in detail in the Holy Qur'ān and Āhadeeth. This book endeavours its readers to help create a bond with Allāh I in attaining His friendship as He is the sole Creator of all material and immaterial things. It is only through Allāh's I friendship, an individual will achieve happiness in this life and the Hereafter, hence eliminate worries, sadness, depression, anxiety and misery of this world.   **UK RRP: £3.00**

Gems & Jewels

This book contains a selection of articles which have been gathered for the benefit of the readers covering a variety of topics on various aspects of daily life. It offers precious advice and anecdotes that contain moral lessons. The advice captivates its readers and will extend the narrowness of their thoughts to deep reflection, wisdom and appreciation of the purpose of our existence.   **UK RRP: £4.00**

End of Time

This book is a comprehensive explanation of the three Sūrahs of Juzz Amma; Sūrah Takweer, Sūrah Infitār and Sūrah Mutaffifeen. This book is a continuation from the previous book of the same author, 'Horrors of Judgement Day'. The three Sūrahs vividly sketch out the scene of the Day of Judgement and describe the state of both the inmates of Jannah and Jahannam. Mufti Saiful Islām Sāhib provides an easy but comprehensive commentary of the three Sūrahs facilitating its understanding for the readers whilst capturing the horrific scene of the ending of the world and the conditions of mankind on that horrific Day.   **UK RRP: £5.00**

Andalus (modern day Spain), the long lost history, was once a country that produced many great calibre of Muslim scholars comprising of Mufassirūn, Muhaddithūn, Fuqahā, judges, scientists, philosophers, surgeons, to name but a few. The Muslims conquered Andalus in 711 AD and ruled over it for eight-hundred years. This was known as the era of Muslim glory. Many non-Muslim Europeans during that time travelled to Spain to study under Muslim scholars. The remanences of the Muslim rule in Spain are manifested through their universities, magnificent palaces and Masājid carved with Arabic writings, standing even until today. In this book, Shaykh Mufti Saiful Islām shares some of his valuable experiences he witnessed during his journey to Spain.   **UK RRP: £3.00**